Leader's Guide

Guided Meditations for Ordinary Time

Leader's Guide

Guided Meditations for Ordinary Time: Courage, Loss, Gratitude, and Needs

Jane E. Ayer

Saint Mary's Press
Christian Brothers Publications
Winona, Minnesota

Genuine recycled paper with 10% post-consumer waste.
Printed with soy-based ink.

The publishing team included Carl Koch, development editor; Rebecca
Fairbank, copy editor; James H. Gurley, production editor and typesetter;
Maurine R. Twait, art director; Elaine Kohner, illustrator; cover photo
copyright © by Liz Hymans, Tony Stone Images; pre-press, printing, and
binding by the graphics division of Saint Mary's Press.

The scriptural text throughout this book is freely adapted. These adaptations
are not to be interpreted or used as official translations of the Scriptures.

The acknowledgments continue on page 51.

Printed in the United States of America

Printing: 9 8 7 6 5 4 3 2 1

Year: 2006 05 04 03 02 01 00 99 98

ISBN 0-88489-586-6

Contents

To Jean,

faithful friend and trusted colleague,

who candidly and lovingly

shared moments of the Sacred with me

during ordinary times,

yet

made them anything but ordinary.

Directions ~~~~~~~~ *for Leading the Meditations*

LEADER
PREPARATION

As the meditation leader, your preparation is especially important to the success of a guided meditation. Pray the meditation before leading a group in it. This will help you to become comfortable with its style and content. Some materials may require a brief doctrinal review with the group. By praying the meditation first, you will become aware if there is a need to do this.

If you choose to have your group do one of the optional art expressions as a follow-up to the meditations, it is best if you try it out before the group gathers to make sure it works well and to know better what directions to give.

If you intend to guide the meditations yourself rather than use the accompanying cassette or compact disc, rehearse the guided prayer, including the introductory comments, the scriptural reading, and the opening and closing prayers, so that appropriate and sufficient time is allowed for the imagery to take place and for prayerful reflection to occur. The meditations should be read slowly and prayerfully, using soft instrumental music as a background.

Only a good reader who has prepared should read aloud the scriptural passage that precedes each guided meditation. The scriptural passage is important to establishing the theme and the tone of the meditation. Read it with reverence and expression, using a Bible.

PARTICIPANT
PREPARATION

To introduce praying a guided meditation, it might be helpful to explain that the participants will be using a prayer form that will call upon their imagination, and that the Holy Spirit graces our imagination during prayer to help us to communicate with God. Remember that this type of prayer may not be easy for everyone in the group. Some may be self-conscious about closing their eyes; some may have difficulty getting in touch with their feelings; some may have personal obstacles in their relationship with God. Sometimes it helps to reassure the participants that if they cannot "get into it" they can use the quiet time to just slow themselves down, relax, and talk to the Lord in their own way. Participants can also be told that although the meditation is guided, if the Spirit leads them in another direction, it is okay for them to go with their own reflection and not worry about the words being spoken. Be gentle, let go, and let the Spirit work.

A possible difficulty, one that may not be apparent at first, may be encountered by those who wear the type of contact lenses that prevent them from closing their eyes for an extended period of time. Invite these participants to put their head down, hiding their eyes in the dark crook of their arm, if they are unable to remove the lenses. Another possible difficulty may be experienced by those who have a sinus problem or asthma. Instead of breathing through their nose during the deep-breathing exercises, they can breathe quietly through their mouth. Also, during the relaxation and centering phases of the meditation, the span of time for holding the breath should be very brief.

MUSIC Quiet instrumental music is important for setting and keeping the mood of the meditation. Music can be playing even as the group gathers. It is a nice background for giving instructions. Have additional tapes or compact discs ready to play during the activities after the guided meditation. Ideally, the follow-up activities will take place in a separate space; therefore, it is less disruptive if cassette or CD players are already set up in the different areas.

REFLECTION QUESTIONS Allowing time for the participants to reflect and name the experiences they have just gone through is a necessary part of these prayer experiences. The reflection questions will help the participants do this successfully. Choose several reflection questions (or use questions similar to them) and type them up, leaving room after each for a response. Make a copy for each participant. Allow enough time for each person to respond to the questions and to share his or her responses with the group. These prayer experiences are not meant to be rushed.

To avoid disrupting the quiet mood of the meditation time, pass out the reflection questions (placed facedown) as the participants take their places. Also give a pen or pencil to each person. If people are sitting on the floor, you could give out hardcover books or clipboards to facilitate writing. Explain that you are distributing reflection questions for use after the meditation.

Assure the participants that their responses are private and that their papers are not going to be collected. When it is time for sharing, honor and affirm all responses, and respect those persons who do not wish to answer aloud.

ART EXPRESSION AND PRAYER RITUAL (OPTIONAL)

Each prayer experience comes with two optional art expressions, each of which contains a prayer ritual. You might choose to use one of these rather than the reflection questions.

If you choose to do one of the optional art expressions, prepare the art materials ahead of time and lay them out in the area where the participants will work. Familiarize the group with the art activity before the prayer time, if possible, so as not to disrupt the meditative mood. This should allow you to give particular directions for the art activity without having to answer a lot of questions. If you have previously completed the art expression, it might be helpful to show your sample artwork at this time.

SETTING

It is imperative that the area for the prayer experience is quiet—no ringing of telephones, bells, and the like. If necessary, put a sign on the outside of your door: Praying! Please do not disturb!

Participants may sit in chairs or find a comfortable position on the floor, but they must be a few feet from one another so that they each have their own space and do not distract one another. Therefore, the area must be large enough so the participants are not crowded. Lying down on the floor should be discouraged, as some participants are likely to fall asleep.

CENTERPIECE (OPTIONAL)

Each theme of the prayer experiences can be enhanced by creating a centerpiece that can be placed on a small table, an altar, or the middle of the floor. The centerpiece should include objects that reflect the message of the prayer. For example, for the meditation on courage ("Take Up Your Mat and Walk"), the centerpiece might consist of a pillow and blanket, a cot, or a child's napping mat; a crutch or cane; a Bible opened to the scriptural passage; and candles—all positioned on a brown or tan cloth.

To set the theme for the meditation on loss ("Lord, If Only You Had Been Here!"), the centerpiece might display candles, incense (be careful of allergies), a makeshift tomb, and a Bible opened to the scriptural passage, all attractively arranged on a gold or white cloth.

A centerpiece for the meditation on gratitude ("Discovered Blessings") might include coins, a dustpan and broom, a treasure chest, candles, and a Bible opened to the scriptural passage, decoratively arranged on a yellow or red cloth.

To enhance the meditation on needs ("Water for the Thirsty"), you might display a wishing well or a pitcher of water and a ladle, candles, and a Bible opened to the scriptural passage, all displayed on a blue cloth.

MATERIALS NEEDED FOR EACH MEDITATION

- a Bible
- an audiotape or CD player
- the meditation recording or script
- tapes or CDs of instrumental music
- reflection questions (a copy for each participant)
- pens or pencils
- clipboards or hardcover books to facilitate writing, if needed
- materials for the art expression (optional; see individual project's needs)
- a centerpiece to reflect the theme (optional)
- a sign that reads Praying! Please do not disturb!

Courage
Take Up Your Mat and Walk

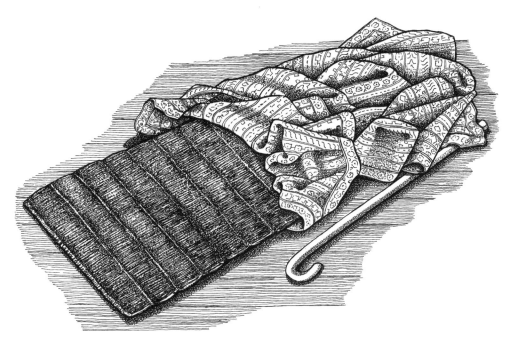

This empowering prayer experience, "Take Up Your Mat and Walk," is based on Jesus' cure of the paralytic. It reminds us that if we have faith in Jesus, he will grace us with the courage to overcome that which immobilizes us. He will bless us with the courage to move toward healthy choices, toward what is life-giving, toward what is essential to our convictions.

THEME   After you have given directions to the participants and set the tone for meditation, introduce the theme by saying something like the following:

> It is critical that we take time in self-reflective prayer to face the areas of our life or personality that immobilize us. Just like the paralyzed man who presented himself to

Jesus through the aid of his friends, we, too, need to find the courage to look honestly into ourselves and present ourselves to Jesus for healing. For us as Christians, the gift of courage is essential in helping us to move toward right choices and toward doing what is good for ourselves and others, despite feelings of fear. If we allow ourselves to come face to face with Jesus and profess our faith in him, then God's grace will give us courage to grow in our weak places and to overcome the obstacles that engender fear and paralysis in us. To do this, we have only to risk entering our quiet place apart.

OPENING   Read aloud this opening prayer:

Compassionate Jesus, we come to you in earnest to face those things, situations, people, and aspects of ourselves that cause fear and paralysis. Gift us with the same faith that belonged to the paralyzed man, so that you will grant us your healing touch. Embrace us with your Spirit so that we may be fearless in presenting to you ourselves and the dark shadows in our life that immobilize us. We ask you to say to each of us, "Get up, take up your mat, and walk," so that as your disciples our lives may be filled with great courage and renewed energy. We say this prayer with firm belief in your healing power. Amen.

SCRIPTURE   Read aloud Mark 2:1–12, using a Bible.

SCRIPT   Play the "Take Up Your Mat and Walk" meditation on the accompanying recording, or slowly and reverently read aloud the following script for the guided meditation. Play soft, instrumental background music.

Today you will enter the hush of your quiet place and meet Jesus in your imagination. First, you will begin by doing some deep-breathing exercises. When I say to, if you can, breathe in and out through your nose very quietly during these exercises. Close your eyes and get comfortable. You will be relaxing your entire body.

Breathe in deeply . . . hold it . . . breathe out slowly and completely. Breathe in deeply . . . hold it . . . breathe out slowly and completely. Again, breathe in deeply . . . hold it . . . breathe out slowly and completely.

Allow your feet and ankles to relax. . . . Relax your legs . . . and your hips. . . . Stay mindful of your breathing. Relax your stomach muscles . . . and now your chest. . . . Just relax. . . . Let your arms grow limp. . . . Relax your wrists, . . . your hands, . . . and your fingers. . . . Keep breathing in deeply and out slowly.

Allow your shoulders to become heavy. . . . Let all the tension drain from your shoulders. . . . Relax your neck, . . . your facial muscles, . . . your forehead, . . . and even your eyelids. . . . Just relax. . . . Breathe in deeply . . . hold it . . . breathe out slowly and completely. [Pause.]

You are in the middle of a crowd just outside a house in which Jesus is visiting. . . . Like those around you, you long to see his face and the action that is going on inside. You have just witnessed a group of people climbing up onto the roof, tearing off part of it. With them, they carried a paralyzed man, and they are about ready to lower him through the roof so that he can get closer to Jesus. . . . Keep moving gently through the crowd so that you can get closer, too. . . .

You make it to the doorway in time to see Jesus' reaction to the man being lowered right in front of his face. Jesus is amused. But others are complaining at the interruption. . . . Jesus simply

lifts up a hand and moves closer to the man. . . .
Jesus is smiling at him, "Your sins are forgiven. . . ."
The paralytic man looks at Jesus gratefully, yet the
whole crowd begins to mumble with accusation.
You see Jesus turn to them and tell them that he
knows what they are thinking. . . . He asks them,
"Do you think it is easier to say 'your sins are forgiven,' or 'get up, take up your mat, and walk'?" . . .
You hear the mumbling continue. . . . Jesus looks
at them, . . . then he says, "So that you will know
who I am . . ." and turning to the paralytic, whose
eyes have never left Jesus' face, he lovingly commands with a powerful authority, "Get up, take up
your mat, and walk." . . .

There are several gasps in the room as the
man rolls onto his side, kneels, and begins to stand.
. . . His friends start to grab him, to help him, . . .
but he motions them to stand back. . . . He
straightens up and everyone cheers! . . . The joy
in the man's face is overwhelming. Those gathered
around him continue to shout at the miracle they
have just witnessed. . . . The noise reaches to
those outside, who start cheering and laughing. . . .
Within the house, some are happily slapping Jesus
on the back, congratulating him. . . . The man
who has been cured reaches toward Jesus to embrace him . . . to thank him. . . . Jesus reaches
out to him in return and hugs him in great joy,
while saying softly to him, "Praise God!" . . .

Jesus leaves the merriment from inside the
house and walks outside where another cheer
erupts. . . . Jesus greets those around him, pro-
claiming again, "Praise God!" . . . The crowd
begins to chant, "Praise God! Praise God!" Then,
as Jesus starts to leave the crowd, he looks around,

searching. . . . Finally, he finds you, . . . gazes directly into your eyes, . . . says your name, . . . and motions for you to come walk with him. . . . The crowd wants to follow, but Jesus shakes his head at them with a gentle no. . . . He wants to be only with you. . . . Notice how you are feeling to have this time alone with him. . . .

As you walk together, Jesus lovingly asks you to share what paralyzes you . . . to name the fears, weaknesses, sins, persons, or problem areas that cripple you. . . . Allow the caring and concern that you hear in Jesus' voice to encourage you to now open up and share all that is in your heart. [Pause.]

Jesus now asks you to name what it is that will give you the courage to face these demons in your life and who are your friends or family that might help you. . . . Answer Jesus. [Pause.]

Then Jesus asks you if you can believe in yourself, for he tells you that he has faith in you. . . . Respond to Jesus. . . . Notice what you are feeling when he tells you that your sins are already forgiven and that you may get up, take up your mat, and walk—with all those things that have paralyzed you before—for you are to be graced with the courage to deal with them. . . . Jesus extends his hands above your head to pray. . . . Listen to his warm, strong, but tender voice as he prays in blessing over you. . . . It will be a prayer of courage just for you. [Pause.]

Notice what you are feeling at this moment. . . .

Your time with Jesus is coming to an end. . . . You can hear the voices of the crowd getting closer. . . . They, too, want to be with Jesus. He looks at you and tells you, "You are not alone. . . . I will be forever with you. . . ." Take a moment to say good-bye and express what is in your heart to Jesus. . . . Allow yourself to feel the hug that Jesus gives you in farewell. . . . Watch him turn and walk to meet the crowd to allow you a few more moments of quiet. . . . Continue walking, and reflect on all that you have shared. . . . Let yourself feel empowered by this time you spent with Jesus. . . .

Breathe in deeply . . . hold it . . . breathe out slowly and completely. Breathe in deeply . . . hold it . . . breathe out slowly and completely. Once more, breathe in deeply . . . hold it . . . breathe out slowly and completely. And when you are ready, you may open your eyes.

REFLECTION   Continue to play instrumental music. Ask the participants to reflect on the experience they have just gone through by pondering some of the following questions or questions similar to these. You might want to suggest that they respond to those questions that speak most to them. Allow time for them to write their reflections.

- What was it like to be part of the crowd longing to see Jesus?
- What did I think of the group of friends lowering the paralyzed man through the roof?
- What was I feeling when I saw Jesus cure the man? hug the man?
- Did I allow myself to get caught up in the emotion of the crowd? Why or why not?
- What did I feel when Jesus looked at me and invited me to walk with him?
- Was I surprised that he knew my name?
- Name the things I shared with Jesus that paralyze me in the way of

- ○ fears . . .
- ○ weaknesses . . .
- ○ sinfulness . . .
- ○ persons . . .
- ○ problem areas . . .
- ○ something else . . .
- • What did I tell Jesus that will give me the courage to face these fears?
- • Who did I name as persons who will help me face my fears?
- • When Jesus prayed over me, did anything he said particularly move me or mean something to me?
- • How did I feel when the crowd was getting closer and my time with Jesus was ending?
- • What was our good-bye like? Could I allow myself to receive the hug that Jesus offered me?
- • In what ways do I feel empowered with courage?
- • What is the special message or image that I will remember from this prayer experience?

Invite and encourage the participants to share their reflections, but do not pressure them to open up. Explain that sharing faith experiences can deepen and strengthen one another's faith, and that they need share only what they are comfortable disclosing to the group. Continue playing instrumental music, as it helps with reverencing the moment. Allow time for the sharing and affirming of each person.

ART EXPRESSION AND PRAYER RITUAL (OPTIONAL)

The art expression and prayer ritual is an optional activity. It can be used in place of the reflection questions. If you decide to use one of these activities, prepare the art area before the group gathers.

After the meditation, continue to play quiet music in the art area. Invite the participants to move quietly to one of the prepared places.

ART EXPRESSION 1   Set a place for each participant with art paper and markers or crayons. Instruct the participants to draw on their art paper two mats or pallets like the one the paralyzed man was lying on. Invite the participants to express on one of the mats how they felt before their meeting with Jesus, by using colors to depict what crippled them. Each color they use should represent a problem area. Then, on the other mat, have them use colors to depict how they felt about the same problem areas *after* their sharing with Jesus.

ART EXPRESSION 2   Set a place for each participant with permanent markers or acrylic or tempera paints and brushes, a 9-by-5-inch sheet of colored plastic (that is, from a roll of plastic tablecloth) or a piece of material, two paper towels, and masking or Scotch tape. If painting is to be done, lay newspaper on the table, and have small cups of water and extra paper towels handy.

Instruct the participants to fashion a mat by wrapping the material or plastic sheet around the folded paper towels and taping the outside covering in place. Have the participants use either markers or paints to decorate their mat with colors, designs, words, or symbols to depict their insights and feelings about what paralyzes them. Have them creatively and freely express what they most want to remember from this prayer experience.

After either art expression, explain to the participants that by sharing our faith experiences, we can help strengthen one another's faith. Then invite them to share the effect the prayer time had on them by explaining the significance of the colors, words, or symbols expressed in their artwork. Add that after they have finished describing their artwork, they are to reverently pass it around from person to person as a sign of being willing to help one another get to Jesus, just as the friends did who lowered the paralytic through the roof. Perhaps they could pray, "Loving Jesus, grace me with courage and healing," or something similar as they begin to pass their art expression around. The rest of the group could pray, "Loving Jesus, grace her [or him] with courage and healing," or something similar each time.

Allow plenty of time for the sharing and affirming of each person. Continue playing instrumental music, as it helps with reverencing the moment. Remind the participants that they can return to their imagination at any time and be in the presence of Jesus in this real way. Encourage them to place their art expression in a visible spot in their home as a reminder of their time spent with Jesus and of the courage he offers them if they believe.

CLOSING   For closure to the meditation experience, have different participants share in reading aloud the following litany of thanksgiving:

Litany Response
Healing God, thank you for courage.

During the times we are face to face with our addictions . . . [All respond.]

When persons threaten us, our self-esteem, or our way of doing things . . . [All respond.]

For those situations in which we must confront something or someone we fear . . . [All respond.]

During those moments when our emotions want to control or immobilize us . . . [All respond.]

At those times when sin is more attractive than following you . . . [All respond.]

When our self-doubt or our lack of self-love inhibits our growth . . . [All respond.]

In those moments when great pain or incredible loss paralyzes us . . . [All respond.]

During the times when our problem areas freeze us from acting decisively or from making good choices . . . [All respond.]

When the way we live diminishes our relationship with you . . . [All respond.]

Invite the participants to add any other prayer intentions. When all have finished, close by praying once more, "Healing God, thank you for courage."

Loss
Lord, If Only You Had Been Here!

This healing prayer experience, "Lord, If Only You Had Been Here!" is based on the pain and grief experienced by Mary, Martha, and Jesus at the death of Lazarus. It reminds us that Jesus, too, feels the anguish of loss, and he offers us his compassion and comfort in the midst of our suffering, no matter what its source.

THEME   After you have given directions to the participants and set the tone for meditation, introduce the theme by saying something like the following:

> Our heart holds many memories that are ravaged by sadness and grief. Yet Jesus offers us the gift of his comfort and peace if we bring our pain to him and take the time to open up and share our wounds by naming our losses aloud to him. Jesus will hold all our hurts and help us to understand and cope with them if we risk and enter our quiet place apart.

OPENING   Read aloud this opening prayer:

> Jesus, you wept at the news of Lazarus's death. You were anguished by the suffering of your friends, Martha and Mary. You entered into the painful experience of profound loss. Yet with your own belief in God, you surmounted grief and chose life instead. Help us also to overcome our grief as we mourn our varied and painful losses, so that we might come to choose what is good and holy and healing for ourselves and those around us. Help us to choose life. You openly shared your humanness with us. Dear Jesus, now grant us the grace that we might share our humanness with you as we examine our losses and profound vulnerabilities. We ask this with belief in your tenderness and compassion. Amen.

SCRIPTURE   Read aloud John 11:1–44, using a Bible.

SCRIPT   Play the "Lord, If Only You Had Been Here!" meditation on the accompanying recording, or slowly and reverently read aloud the following script for the guided meditation. Play soft, instrumental background music.

> Today you will enter the hush of your quiet place and meet Jesus in your imagination. First, you will begin by doing some deep-breathing exercises. When I say to, if you can, breathe in and out through your nose very quietly during these exercises. Close your eyes and get comfortable. You will be relaxing your entire body.
>
> Breathe in deeply . . . hold it . . . breathe out slowly and completely. Breathe in deeply . . . hold it . . . breathe out slowly and completely. Again, breathe in deeply . . . hold it . . . breathe out slowly and completely.
>
> Allow your feet and ankles to relax. . . . Relax your legs . . . and your hips. . . . Stay mindful of your breathing. Relax your stomach

muscles . . . and now your chest. . . . Just relax.
. . . Let your arms grow limp. . . . Relax your
wrists, . . . your hands, . . . and your fingers.
. . . Keep breathing in deeply and out slowly.

Allow your shoulders to become heavy. . . .
Let all the tension drain from your shoulders. . . .
Relax your neck, . . . your facial muscles, . . .
your forehead, . . . and even your eyelids. . . .
Just relax. . . . Breathe in deeply . . . hold it . . .
breathe out slowly and completely. [Pause.]

Today you are in Jerusalem. . . . The sky is
a brilliant blue and cloudless. . . . The dust lies
low, as there is no breeze this day. Although the sun
is somewhat hot, you hardly notice, for you are
with Jesus. He is only a little ahead of you, sur-
rounded by a crowd of his followers who press
forward to get closer to him. . . . You know that
Jesus is somewhat fatigued, and you wonder how he
can keep up the intensity with which he preaches
and touches people. . . . Even now his hand
moves to rest on the shoulder of a beggar. . . .
You have been a witness to his powerful presence
over and over these last few days. . . . It is clear
that many of those around you are on fire with his
words. . . . You have even overheard people say
that they would put their life in his hands.

Suddenly there is a commotion as a messen-
ger hails Jesus. . . . It seems a friend of his has
died. . . . People near you are repeating over and
over, "It's Lazarus—he's talking about Lazarus! . . ."
You look at Jesus. . . . You see pain momentarily
contort his gentle face. . . . Jesus can barely speak.
. . . Notice what you are feeling to see his grief. . . .

Jesus does not travel to see his grieving friends
right away, so some people near you wonder if he
truly cares about them. . . . But you notice how

often his head turns in the direction of Bethany, and how his eyes mist up with sadness, so you don't need to wonder. . . .

Finally you hear Jesus announce that he is going back to Bethany in Judea. . . . This upsets the crowd, for it was in that same country that Jesus' enemies almost stoned him. . . . Jesus quiets the crowd. . . . You hear him say something about how in the light no one stumbles, but in the night with no light as a guide, one stumbles often. . . . All you know is that Jesus is light to you, . . . and you want to follow him.

You walk the distance back to Bethany with Jesus. . . . Whenever you catch sight of him in the crowd, his face is always filled with sorrow and concentration. . . . You wonder what he is thinking. . . . [Pause.]

When you arrive in Bethany, there is something sadly familiar to you as you enter and witness the sorrow and grieving that is starting to surround you. . . . You think, "Pain looks the same on everybody." . . . People rush to greet Jesus and to fill him in on the details. . . . You see a woman push through them to get to Jesus. . . . She almost stumbles, but does not slow down. . . . Her face is filled with longing. Her breathing is deep and heavy. Jesus reaches out to steady her. . . . Jesus says her name, "Martha." . . . His hand touches her cheek. . . . Jesus asks her quietly, "Where is Mary?" . . .

Martha does not answer, instead she is speaking with such pain and urgency, "Lord, if only you had been here!" . . . Is there anything about which you think, "Lord, if only you had been here?" . . .

Jesus says to Martha, "Whoever lives and believes in me will never die. Do you believe this?" . . . Martha answers, "Yes, Lord." . . . Do *you* believe this?

Another woman is running toward Jesus. . . . A crowd races to keep up with her, but they let her reach him first. . . . She falls to his feet, weeping. . . . She cries out the same thing that her sister did, "Lord, if only you had been here!" . . . She is sobbing so hard. And the people who are with her are crying as well. "Mary." . . . Jesus tries to comfort her, but her anguish is too raw. You look from her to Jesus. . . . His face fills with his own pain and with pain for her. . . . He sighs sadly, holding back his own tears, but then you hear him ask, "Where have you put him?" . . .

"Lord, come and see!" . . . Jesus begins weeping openly now. . . . How do you feel to see Jesus weeping? . . . As you walk toward the tomb, some are saying, "See how much he loved him. . . ." Others are saying, "He could have saved him. . . ."

Jesus stops before the tomb. . . . Jesus commands that the stone be rolled away. . . . Some in the crowd groan with fear, and others gasp with hope. . . . Hear Martha tell Jesus of her concern about the smell of his dead body. . . . Jesus looks long at Martha. . . . He asks her, "Have I not told you that if you believe you will see the glory of God?" . . . Jesus raises his face to heaven and prays: "God of heaven and earth, I thank you for having heard me. I know you have always heard me." . . . Jesus now faces the tomb. . . . He loudly calls out his friend's name: "Lazarus! Lazarus, my friend! Come out! Go free! . . ."

With your own eyes, you see the man, bound in his grave cloths, come out of the tomb. . . . Everyone hurries to take care of him. . . . There is much hugging, shouting, and crying, but it is of a different sort now. . . . Having seen this miracle, you begin to walk away from the crowd. . . . You reflect on the burden of your own grief. . . . Your head is down as you walk. . . . You watch the ground as you leave. . . . Then right beside you, you notice a pair of sandals keeping step with you. . . . Jesus has come to be with you. . . . You look at him tentatively. . . . There is no fatigue in his face. . . . He is totally present to you. . . . His eyes are loving you as he asks what it is that keeps you in the tomb . . . what are the losses that weigh you down . . . that sometimes make you feel like you're dying inside. . . . You think of the words that Martha and Mary spoke, "Lord, if only you had been here." . . .

Allow your pain to surface. . . . Take Jesus to your tomb. . . . It is the moment to say to him, "Lord, come and see. . . ." Use this time to share with Jesus all for which your heart mourns. Know that he will share your hurting. [Pause.]

Listen to his words and feel his love as Jesus offers you wisdom and comfort. . . . It is okay if you need Jesus to hold you. . . . [Pause.]

You have walked back in front of the tomb—Lazarus's tomb—your tomb. The stone has been rolled away. The tomb is empty. Jesus takes your hand and reminds you that it is he to whom you must come in your heartache, and he will help you roll away the stone each time. . . . Jesus says these words to you, "Did I not tell you that if you believe in me, you will never die . . . that you will see the glory of God? . . ." Allow yourself to respond to Jesus with what you are thinking and feeling. . . . [Pause.]

It is time for Jesus to return to his friends. He tells you that he is glad to have had this time together with you. . . . Still holding your hand in his, hear Jesus say, "Let us pray. . . ." Out of the corner of your eye, you see him lift his face to heaven. . . . Then you do, too. Listen to his prayer. He is praying for you. [Pause.]

Express your good-bye in whatever way is comfortable for you . . . and then let Jesus return to the others. . . . [Pause.]

Continue walking on your way. . . . Allow peace to settle over you and through you . . . for you have shared your losses and all for which your heart mourns. . . . And Jesus who loves you has taken time to walk with your sadness, . . . to roll back the stone of your dark tomb, . . . and to set you free to choose life. . . .

Breathe in deeply . . . hold it . . . breathe out slowly and completely. Breathe in deeply . . . hold it . . . breathe out slowly and completely. Once more, breathe in deeply . . . hold it . . . breathe out slowly and completely. And when you are ready, you may open your eyes.

REFLECTION Continue to play instrumental music. Ask the participants to reflect on the experience they have just gone through by pondering some of the following questions or questions similar to these. You might want to suggest that they respond to those questions that speak most to them. Allow time for them to write their reflections.

• What was it like to be in Jerusalem in the crowd walking with Jesus?

- What did I hear people saying about him? Did I feel the same way?
- How did Jesus' emotions change when he heard of the death of Lazarus? How was I affected by Jesus' grief?
- How did I deal with the pain of Mary, Martha, and the crowd? Did it bring personal pain to the surface for me? If so, what was the pain about?
- Did Jesus' question, "Have I not told you that if you believe you will see the glory of God?" raise any thoughts or feelings for me?
- Was there anything for which I thought, "Lord, if only you had been here"?
- What was I thinking and feeling as Jesus commanded Lazarus to come out of the tomb?
- Could I allow myself to be happy for Lazarus's family and the crowd?
- What was my reaction when I noticed Jesus walking beside me?
- Was it difficult for me to share all for which my heart mourns? Why or why not?
- What are my losses that make me sad?
- What does Jesus offer me for wisdom and comfort?
- Did I need Jesus to hold me? If so, how did it feel?
- How do I feel having shared with Jesus?
- How did it feel to have Jesus take my hand in his?
- Could I believe in the words of Jesus, "If you believe in me, you will never die, and you will see the glory of God"? If so, in what ways do those words help me deal with my losses?
- What was the prayer that Jesus prayed for me?
- Did I experience my stone being rolled away, and myself being set free to choose life? Explain.
- What is the special message or image that I will remember from this prayer experience?

Invite and encourage the participants to share their reflections, but do not pressure them to open up. Explain that sharing faith experiences can deepen and strengthen one another's faith, and that they need share only what they are comfortable disclosing to the group. Continue playing instrumental music, as it helps with reverencing the moment. Allow time for the sharing and affirming of each person.

ART EXPRESSION AND PRAYER RITUAL (OPTIONAL)

The art expression and prayer ritual is an optional activity. It can be used in place of the reflection questions. If you decide to use one of these activities, prepare the art area before the group gathers.

For a smokeless fire for the prayer ritual at the conclusion of the sharing, have prepared a 4-quart heavy pot with a cover. Empty a box of salt into the pot. Also have ready a bottle of rubbing alcohol, a wooden spoon, and matches. Although this fire will be smokeless, it will burn extremely hot, so place a brick or piece of slate under the pan to protect the rug or flooring. Be careful when doing this activity in a small room with a smoke detector—the heat may set it off. The cover for the pot should be nearby.

After the meditation, continue to play quiet music in the art area. Invite the participants to move to one of the prepared places.

ART EXPRESSION 1

Set each place with a paper plate, markers or crayons, a pen or pencil, and a slip of paper.

Direct the participants to express their feelings of loss and grief from before and after their meeting with Jesus by using splashes of color or designs. Tell them that the colors they choose should be symbolic of the emotions they felt and are feeling about their losses. They may use words or other symbols if they care to do so.

Then tell the participants to write on their slip of paper all the losses that they would like to lift up to Jesus so that the pain associated with these losses may continue to diminish.

ART EXPRESSION 2 Cover the art table(s) with newspaper. Set a place for each participant with a large stone or rock, poster or acrylic paints, a paintbrush, a small cup of water, and paper towels. Also give each person a pen or pencil and a slip of paper.

Direct the participants to paint part of their rock using colors depicting how they felt about their losses *before* their time with Jesus, and to paint the rest of their rock using colors depicting how they felt *after* their time with Jesus. Or they may decorate their rock to symbolize anything meaningful to them from their prayer experience.

Then have the participants write on their slip of paper all the losses that they would like to lift up to Jesus so that the pain associated with these losses may continue to diminish.

After either art expression, explain that by sharing our faith experiences, we can help strengthen one another's faith. Then invite the participants to share the effect the prayer time had on them by explaining the significance of the colors and symbolism expressed in their artwork. Add that after they have finished describing their art expression, they are to place it in the middle of the prayer circle (or another designated place). Then they are to place their folded slip of paper into the pan you have prepared in readiness for burning. Perhaps they could pray, "Jesus, hold my losses, diminish my pain," or something similar as they set their artwork down or place their slips of paper in the pot to be burned.

Once the participants have put their slips of paper in the pot of salt, pour in 1/2 to 2/3 of the alcohol and stir, using the wooden spoon. The papers should become at least partially covered with some of the salt and alcohol mixture. Drop in a lit match to start the fire. *Should you have any safety concerns during the burning, simply put the cover on the pot.*

After the fire ritual, allow plenty of time for the sharing and affirming of each person. Continue playing instrumental music, as it helps with reverencing the moment. Remind the participants that they can return to their imagination at any time and be with Jesus in this very real way. Suggest that they place their artwork in a visible spot at home to remind them that they are not alone in their grieving, that Jesus helps them hold their grief and offers them life, love, peace, and joy.

CLOSING

For closure to the meditation experience, lead the following prayer of petition:

> *Litany Response*
> Loving Jesus, be here in our sorrow . . . help us to choose life.
>
> For all who mourn the death of loved ones, whether from accident, violence, or natural causes . . . [All respond.]
>
> For all who have lost relationships due to fights, mis-understandings, divorce, or for other reasons . . . [All respond.]
>
> For all who grieve because of infertility, miscarriage, or abortion . . . [All respond.]
>
> For all who are suffering due to unemployment or to a loss of income, a residence, or insurance . . . [All respond.]
>
> For all who struggle to find or maintain their faith . . . [All respond.]
>
> For all who suffer loneliness because of lack of contact with or sensitivity from family members . . . [All respond.]
>
> For all who anguish because someone they love has been abducted or lost and has not been found or recov-ered . . . [All respond.]
>
> For all who have lost their sense of trust . . . [All respond.]

For all who are anxious due to health problems . . . [All respond.]

For all who grieve for missing military or other personnel in foreign countries . . . [All respond.]

For all who have lost their way, mentally or emotionally, and who need to reclaim their self-concept, their self-love, and their dreams . . . [All respond.]

For all who suffer the loss of sobriety but still seek what is good and holy and healthy to sustain themselves . . . [All respond.]

For all who need to experience hope again . . . [All respond.]

Gratitude
Discovered Blessings

This enlightening prayer experience, "Discovered Blessings," is based on the parable of the lost coin. It reminds us that we must open ourselves to an awareness of God's constant benevolence, and that we must fully express our gratitude to this gracious God of ours in the same manner that the woman in Jesus' story expressed her gratefulness when she recovered her lost treasure.

THEME   After you have given directions to the participants and set the tone for meditation, introduce the theme by saying something like the following:

> Expressing a sincere gratefulness to our loving God for both the significant and seemingly insignificant persons, events, and situations that surround us is extremely valuable because it connects us to the living movements

of God in our life. God's flow of daily gifts to us is so magnanimous that we must invite into ourselves the spirit of surprise so that nothing will be taken for granted. Developing a grateful heart helps us to recognize the joys in the midst of our struggles, as well as to acknowledge the opportunities for growth that are present in the difficult challenges we face. This sense of gratitude for both hidden and apparent blessings can evolve if we risk to enter our quiet place apart.

OPENING   Read aloud this opening prayer:

Loving God, just as the woman in your parable expressed her thankfulness for finding her coin, help us during this prayer time to be open to what is good in our life, no matter how insignificant it seems. Guide us in naming our troubles so that we may look at them as potential gifts and blessings. Allow this time to raise our awareness of your loving presence and movement in our life and of the treasures with which you constantly bless us. We ask this in the spirit of the woman in your story. Amen.

SCRIPTURE   Read aloud Luke 15:8, using a Bible.

SCRIPT   Play the "Discovered Blessings" meditation on the accompanying recording, or slowly and reverently read aloud the following script for the guided meditation. Play soft, instrumental background music.

Today you will enter the hush of your quiet place and meet Jesus in your imagination. First, you will begin by doing some deep-breathing exercises. When I say to, if you can, breathe in and out through your nose very quietly during these exercises. Close your eyes and get comfortable. You will be relaxing your entire body.

Breathe in deeply . . . hold it . . . breathe out slowly and completely. Breathe in deeply . . . hold it . . . breathe out slowly and completely. Again, breathe in deeply . . . hold it . . . breathe out slowly and completely.

Allow your feet and ankles to relax. . . . Relax your legs . . . and your hips. . . . Stay mindful of your breathing. Relax your stomach muscles . . . and now your chest. . . . Just relax. . . . Let your arms grow limp. . . . Relax your wrists, . . . your hands, . . . and your fingers. . . . Keep breathing in deeply and out slowly.

Allow your shoulders to become heavy. . . . Let all the tension drain from your shoulders. . . . Relax your neck, . . . your facial muscles, . . . your forehead, . . . and even your eyelids. . . . Just relax. . . . Breathe in deeply . . . hold it . . . breathe out slowly and completely. [Pause.]

You are a quiet bystander in the doorway of the woman's cottage. She is not aware of your presence, for she is frantic. She has lost something very valuable to her, so she is moving chairs and the table and looking all around the floor under each of them. . . . She walks back and forth now, from one end of the room to the other, with her hands clasped over her head, which she keeps shaking in disbelief. . . . She does this several times and then begins to moan, covering her mouth and rocking back and forth on her feet. . . . Taking a deep breath, she continues looking. She grabs a broom from the corner and begins to sweep. . . . Achingly, slowly, she bends over and lifts a corner of the worn rug in the center of the room. . . . She cries with delight as she reaches lower to pick up the dust-covered coin. . . . With one hand on her broom and the other clutched around her coin, she raises herself up with joy. . . . Now with both hands in the air, one clasped around her broom and the other one still closed tightly around her treasure, she dances with happiness. . . . Her joy is great! She is praising God with her voice and in her dancing. . . .

You turn away from the door now and walk over to and sit upon a stone wall near her cottage. . . . You think about the things, events, or people for which you are most grateful. . . . Are there seemingly insignificant moments or persons that you have let slip by you without acknowledging them? Let your mind fill with what is good in your life, and allow your heart to sing with gratitude to the Most High for God's loving movements in your life. [Pause.]

You turn your head as you hear footsteps crunching the gravel and coming toward you. . . . It is Jesus! He greets you by name and asks if he may join you on your stone wall. . . . There is such a warmth about him, and a joy, too. . . . He tells you that he is grateful to have time alone with you. . . . How does it feel to hear this from Jesus?

Jesus looks at you steadily and says quietly, "Your heart is full." . . . Begin sharing with Jesus the people, things, and situations for which you are grateful. [Pause.]

Jesus simply responds, "God is good!" . . . Next, he invites you to share some of the troubled areas in your life so that you appreciate the ways in which you can grow during these times and become more aware of who you are—created in the Most High's image. . . .

Take this time to talk with Jesus and discover how you can even be grateful for the difficulties you face. [Pause.]

Listen as Jesus reminds you that God's joy at having you close in times of difficulty is like the woman's joy in finding her lost treasure. . . . Jesus tells you, "You are a great blessing to me and to all who love you." . . . Allow yourself to feel his words warm you. . . .

Jesus tells you that it is important to reflect in gratitude on each day before laying your head on the pillow . . . that praising and giving thanks to the Most High should become a natural part of your life. . . . Jesus encourages you to do this in daily prayer or through keeping a gratitude journal. . . . It is something for you to think about.

Jesus turns toward you and takes both of your hands in his. Hear him say, "I want to pray in thanksgiving with you." . . . Together you bow your heads. . . . Listen to Jesus' prayer for you. Warmly, he says your name, squeezing your hands gently in his. . . . With his words, he blesses you in gratitude for the good you do, . . . for your courage to open up and discover what can become positive in your troubled areas, . . . and for your thankfulness in acknowledging the Most High's movements in your life. . . . Hear him as he wishes you peace and a grateful heart always. . . . Does he say anything else to you? [Pause.]

You and Jesus look into each other's eyes. . . . It has been a special visit together, but it is time for Jesus to go now. Take time to say good-bye in a way that expresses what you are feeling. [Pause.]

Watch as Jesus walks through the village and out of sight. . . . Sit quietly on the stone wall and remember your reflections and your sharings with Jesus. . . . Reflect on any plans that will aid you in being more consciously grateful for the persons, moments, or situations that make up your world. . . . Remember, too, the effort it will take to look differently at the troubled areas so that they can be viewed as opportunities of change and growth and thereby, be hidden blessings. . . . What will be your plan—a prayer at night? . . . a gratitude journal? . . . a note put up in your home to remember to praise and thank the Most High daily? . . . Remain in the quiet and develop your plan of gratitude. . . . [Pause.]

Breathe in deeply . . . hold it . . . breathe out slowly and completely. Breathe in deeply . . . hold it . . . breathe out slowly and completely. Once more, breathe in deeply . . . hold it . . . breathe out slowly and completely. And when you are ready, you may open your eyes.

REFLECTION
Continue to play instrumental music. Ask the participants to reflect on the experience they have just gone through by pondering some of the following questions or questions similar to these. You might want to suggest that they respond to those questions that speak most to them. Allow time for them to write their reflections.

- What was my reaction to watching the woman frantically look for what she had lost, find the coin, and express great joy and gratefulness in its discovery?
- What were my reflections as I began to think about the big and little things, events, or people in my life that are good? Did any of my thoughts surprise me?
- How did I feel to have Jesus come, greet me by name, sit beside me, and tell me that he was grateful for having time alone with me?

- When Jesus said to me, "Your heart is full," what things for which I am most grateful did I share with Jesus?
- Could I agree with Jesus when he simply said, "God is good!" Why or why not?
- What were the troubled areas of my life that I spoke about to Jesus? Was it easy or hard for me to name opportunities for self-growth and to see my troubles as hidden blessings? What opportunities or hidden blessings did I name?
- Do I feel more confidence and courage now that I have looked at these situations as potential blessings of personal growth and self-discovery?
- What was my inner response when Jesus encouraged me to thank God before I lay my head on the pillow each night?
- What went on inside me when Jesus told me that God's joy in having me close in times of difficulty is like the woman's joy in finding her lost treasure? Did I believe Jesus?
- How did I feel when Jesus took my hands in his and prayed for me? Did anything especially touch me in his prayer? If so, what?
- Was my heart indeed full when I said good-bye to Jesus? How did I express myself?
- Did the woman in the cottage teach me anything? If so, what?
- Did Jesus teach me anything? If so, what?
- Can I promise to be more consciously aware of and grateful for the seemingly insignificant moments, persons, and situations in my life, as well as the obviously significant ones? How will I do this?
- Am I more apt to look with new eyes at the challenges or troubled areas of my life and see them as opportunities for thanksgiving? Explain.
- In what way did I express my good-byes and my feelings to Jesus? How did I feel about his leaving?
- What is the plan I chose to use to express my gratefulness to the Most High? Will I do it in a prayer before sleep?

- Will I write in my journal about God's movement in my life? What will I do?
- What is the special message or image that I will remember from this prayer experience?

Invite and encourage the participants to share their reflections, but do not pressure them to open up. Explain that sharing faith experiences can deepen and strengthen one another's faith, and that they need share only what they are comfortable disclosing to the group. Continue playing instrumental music, as it helps with reverencing the moment. Allow time for the sharing and affirming of each person.

ART EXPRESSION AND PRAYER RITUAL (OPTIONAL)

The art expression and prayer ritual is an optional activity. It can be used in place of the reflection questions. If you decide to use one of these activities, prepare the art area before the group gathers.

After the meditation, continue to play quiet music in the art area. Invite the participants to move to one of the prepared places.

Art Expression 1

Set a place for each participant with yellow or gold construction paper, a compass or large round object for tracing circles, and crayons or makers.

Instruct the participants to draw or trace their "found coin" in the center of the construction paper. Have them decorate their coin by using splashes of color or designs to depict their areas of gratefulness (big and little) and the opportunities for self-growth and thanksgiving they have discovered in their difficulties. If needed, certain colors can denote areas that they may still feel hesitant about claiming as opportunities for gratefulness. Encourage them to share their discovered blessings.

Art Expression 2

Set a place for each participant with a small notebook, a blank book, or several stapled pages in booklet form with a construction paper cover.

Instruct the participants to decorate the cover or first page of their gratitude journal with colors that reflect their time with Jesus and the things for which they are grateful. On a separate page, invite them to write today's date and to express what they named as grateful moments—both clearly significant and seemingly insignificant—and as opportunities for self-growth and gratitude in the midst of troubled areas.

After either art project, explain that by sharing our faith experiences, we can help strengthen one another's faith. Then invite the participants to share the effect that the prayer time had on them by explaining the significance of the colors and any other symbolism in their artwork, or highlights from their gratitude journal. Add that after they have finished sharing, they are to raise their artwork or journal high and then place it in the treasure chest (or some other designated area) as a symbol of the gratitude being expressed. Perhaps they could pray, "Gracious God, I thank you for all that is," or something similar as they lift their art expression or journal up to the Most High.

Allow plenty of time for the sharing and affirming of each person. Continue playing instrumental music, as it helps with reverencing the moment. Remind the participants that they can return to their imagination at any time and be with Jesus in this very real way. Encourage them to place their art expression or journal in a visible spot in their home as a reminder of their pledge to be more gratefully conscious of God's gracious movement in their life.

CLOSING For closure to the meditation experience, slowly, joyfully lead the following litany of thanksgiving:

> *Litany Response*
> Receive our grateful hearts, O gracious God.
>
> For the obvious persons and moments of joy that grace us . . . [All respond.]

For the seemingly insignificant persons and events in our life that we fail to appreciate . . . [All respond.]

For the opportunities of self-discovery and growth that occur in the midst of difficult times . . . [All respond.]

For the parable of the lost coin that teaches us to seek out that which we value and to delight in our treasures as blessings from you . . . [All respond.]

For the uneventful occurrences that knit together the hours of our days . . . [All respond.]

For all situations that we rarely acknowledge with appreciation . . . [All respond.]

For all that has been, is, and will be . . . [All respond.]

The participants can be invited to name additional areas of gratefulness. When all have finished sharing, have the group respond once more with, "Receive our grateful hearts, O Gracious God."

Needs
Water for the Thirsty

This enriching prayer experience, "Water for the Thirsty," is based on the Scripture passage in which Jesus meets the woman at the well. It reminds us that our needs are known, recognized, and met by Jesus, and that Jesus sees past the clutter of our life into our heart and soul. He holds out to us the same life-giving water, which is ours for the taking if we are honest about who we are and what we need.

THEME   After you have given directions to the participants and set the tone for meditation, introduce the theme by saying something like the following:

> Prayer is an important resource for each of us in discovering and naming our needs. It affords us the opportunity to grow quiet, sit with the clutter of our life, and honestly lift our needs to Christ, who loves us and

presents us with himself—life-giving water. We can receive this water if we gently and honestly enter our quiet place apart.

OPENING Read aloud this opening prayer:

Loving Jesus, you took time with the woman at the well. Please take time with us now during this prayer experience. Empower us to be open and to risk by acknowledging the clutter we have made of our life and by naming our personal, inner needs. As you look past our clutter and love us unconditionally, grant us the necessary trust in you so that we will be able to give over our needs for you to hold. Like water for the thirsty, quench the parched areas of our life that only you can replenish. We lift this prayer up to you with confidence. Amen.

SCRIPTURE Read aloud John 4:4–26, using a Bible.

SCRIPT Play the "Water for the Thirsty" meditation on the accompanying recording, or slowly and reverently read aloud the following script for the guided meditation. Play soft, instrumental background music.

Today you will enter the hush of your quiet place and meet Jesus in your imagination. First, you will begin by doing some deep-breathing exercises. When I say to, if you can, breathe in and out through your nose very quietly during these exercises. Close your eyes and get comfortable. You will be relaxing your entire body.

Breathe in deeply . . . hold it . . . breathe out slowly and completely. Breathe in deeply . . . hold it . . . breathe out slowly and completely. Again, breathe in deeply . . . hold it . . . breathe out slowly and completely.

Allow your feet and ankles to relax. . . . Relax your legs . . . and your hips. . . . Stay mindful of your breathing. Relax your stomach muscles . . . and now your chest. . . . Just relax. . . . Let your arms grow limp. . . . Relax your wrists, . . . your hands, . . . and your fingers. . . . Keep breathing in deeply and out slowly.

Allow your shoulders to become heavy. . . . Let all the tension drain from your shoulders. . . . Relax your neck, . . . your facial muscles, . . . your forehead, . . . and even your eyelids. . . . Just relax. . . . Breathe in deeply . . . hold it . . . breathe out slowly and completely. [Pause.]

You are safely alone and carrying a bucket and ladle. . . . You are approaching the well on the outskirts of town. . . . It is hot, and you feel moisture beading up on your face. . . . You reach the well and peer over its side. . . . The coolness of its stone depth and stored water caresses your face. Reach for the hanging rope and release it hand over hand until you have successfully lowered the well's bucket into the water. . . . Slip it in deeply and fill it with as much as you think you can pull up. . . . Using the rope on the pulley again, raise the bucket from the well until you can grab it. . . . Slowly, fill your own bucket and allow yourself the pleasure of hearing the water splash into your pail. . . . Hook the rope back into place, and fill your ladle with cool water. . . . Lift it to your lips and drink in the sparkling liquid. . . . Throw some water onto your face to cool you. . . .

As you straighten up from your bucket, notice a man walking toward the well. . . . You are about to leave when he calls you by name. . . . You recognize the man. He is Jesus of Nazareth. He looks hot and tired. . . . As he nears, he asks if you will share a drink of your water with him. . . .

Notice what you are feeling as you fill your ladle and pass it full and dripping to Jesus. . . . He thankfully acknowledges your kindness with a weary smile before drinking the water. . . . As he drinks, you see his face begin to brighten. . . .

When he finishes, he returns the ladle and invites you to sit with him on the edge of the well. . . . There is some shade provided by its roof, so you agree. . . .

Jesus tells you about your life. . . . Quietly, he names what troubles you . . . what you are not proud of . . . what you wish you could change . . . what your needs are. . . . There is no judgment in his knowing. He speaks with tenderness. Allow yourself to now examine the dark, frustrating, or painful areas of your life with Jesus' help. [Pause.]

See the caring and compassion that Jesus offers you as he tells you that he is life-giving water. . . . He is what you need. . . . Allow yourself to drink in his words, his presence, his strength. . . .

Jesus now asks you to share positive choices that you can act on to make your life better . . . to name what will help you to move toward wholeness and peace with his help. [Pause.]

Jesus affirms you and your course of action. . . . He offers words of encouragement. [Pause.]

Jesus now moves off the side of the well and stands in front of you. . . . He places his two, warm, strong but gentle hands upon your shoulders. . . . Feel the warmth of his hands. . . . He is pouring his Spirit within you. . . . His Spirit will refresh your spirit . . . like water for the thirsty. . . .

He passes you the ladle full of fresh water to drink. . . . He then dips his hands into the cool water of your bucket and touches your face. . . . your cheek, . . . your lips, . . . your eyes, . . . your hands. . . . Listen as Jesus tells you that he wants you to remember this moment as a sign that he is life-giving water, . . . that he is with you always to refresh you, . . . and that your needs are answered in him. . . .

Jesus looks lovingly into your eyes. . . . Quietly, he tells you one more thing. . . . What does he tell you? It is something that you will hold deeply in your heart. [Pause.]

It is time for Jesus to go. . . . Express whatever you are thinking and feeling as you say your good-byes together. . . .

Sit back on the edge of the well and watch as Jesus returns from the direction in which he came. . . . Silently reflect on the needs in your life that you and Jesus examined, and remember his words that he is life-giving water . . . and that he offers this to you. . . .

Breathe in deeply . . . hold it . . . breathe out slowly and completely. Breathe in deeply . . . hold it . . . breathe out slowly and completely. Once more, breathe in deeply . . . hold it . . . breathe out slowly and completely. And when you are ready, you may open your eyes.

REFLECTION Continue to play instrumental music. Ask the participants to reflect on the experience they have just gone through by pondering some of the following questions or questions similar to these. You might want to suggest that they respond to the questions that speak most to them. Allow time for them to write their reflections.

- What was it like for me to be carrying a bucket and ladle to the town well on a hot day?
- How did I feel when Jesus asked me for a drink?
- Was it difficult for me to agree to stay and sit on the side of the well with Jesus?
- What did Jesus tell me about myself? How did I feel while hearing this from him?
- Was it painful to be honest with myself about the clutter of my life? Explain.
- Do I now know more clearly what my needs are? If so, what are they? If not, what keeps them unclear?
- Could I allow myself to feel Jesus' hands on my shoulders and his blessing in my heart? Explain.
- Did I allow myself to drink in his Spirit, his strength, his presence? If so, how will I let this make a difference in my life?
- In what way did I express my good-bye to Jesus?
- Was it hard to see Jesus leave me? Why or why not?
- Do I believe that I can more easily approach Jesus, who is life-giving water, with my needs? Explain.
- What is the special message or image that I will remember from this prayer experience?

Invite and encourage the participants to share their reflections, but do not pressure them to open up. Explain that sharing faith experiences can deepen and strengthen one another's faith, and that they need share only what they are comfortable disclosing to the group. Continue playing instrumental music, as it helps with reverencing the moment. Allow time for the sharing and affirming of each person.

ART EXPRESSION AND PRAYER RITUAL (OPTIONAL)

The art expression and prayer ritual is an optional activity. It can be used in place of the reflection questions. If you decide to use one of these activities, prepare the art area before the group gathers.

After the meditation, continue playing quiet music in the art area. Invite the participants to move to one of the prepared places.

Art Expression 1   Set a place for each participant with a sheet of art paper, crayons or markers, and pencils.

Direct the participants to draw, in the middle of the art paper, the bucket, ladle, or well from the scene with Jesus. Invite them to decorate their ladle, bucket, or well by depicting what needs have been addressed by their meeting with Jesus. This can be done by using just splashes or designs of color that express a particular emotion or need. Or the participants may choose to use words or other symbols.

Art Expression 2   Set a place for each participant with an empty tin can, Popsicle sticks, glue, a 5-by-5-inch piece of brown or tan construction paper (optional), small slips of paper, an 8-inch piece of string or yarn, a 5-by-12-inch piece of foil, a 3-inch piece of wire, and a pen. Have scissors or utility knives available.

Instruct the participants to arrange Popsicle sticks vertically around their can and glue them to the can so that the can is completely covered and they have their own personal well. Then tell them to glue two sticks across from each other at least halfway up the can. Across those two sticks, have them glue one stick horizontally to form the beginning of the roof.

The participants may complete their roof either by placing their construction paper folded and cut to size over this "beam" or by gluing sticks (cut in half) out from this "beam" at an angle. Have them cut one more stick in half and glue it crosswise to the middle of the main beam. The string and bucket will hang from this stick. Show the participants how to form a bucket out of the piece of foil, use the wire to make the handle, and tie the string to it and to the crossbeam of the well. Then instruct the participants to reflectively write on a piece of paper the needs that they shared with Jesus and to drop the paper into their well as a reminder that Jesus offers them life-giving water to fill their needs.

After either art expression, explain that by sharing our faith experiences, we can help strengthen one another's faith. Then invite the participants to share the effect the prayer time had on them by explaining the symbolism of their artwork. Add that after they have finished describing their artwork, they are to place it in the middle of the prayer circle (or another designated place) and receive a blessing. The facilitator (or another assigned person) can dip her or his hand into a bucket of water (which might be part of the centerpiece) and gently place a drop of water on the forehead or palms of each participant after she or he is done sharing. During this anointing ritual, perhaps the facilitator or designated person could say: "Remember, Jesus is life-giving water. Trust that he will fill your needs," or something similar.

Allow plenty of time for the sharing and affirming of each person. Continue playing instrumental music, as it helps with reverencing the moment. Remind the participants that they can return to their imagination at any time and be with Jesus in this very real way and draw on him as life-giving water. Encourage them to place their art expression in a visible spot in their home to remind them of Jesus' presence.

CLOSING   For closure to the meditation experience, slowly and quietly read aloud the following prayer:

> Jesus, you are water for the thirsty. . . . Thank you for giving us a drink during this special time in our quiet place apart. Help us always to come to you with our needs and longings, for we believe that you will hold us in the midst of our clutter. Yes, with certainty you know us and love us regardless of our life story—just as you knew and loved the woman at the well. And as with her, you offer us what you know we need the most—life-giving water. May your Spirit keep alive in us the awareness that it is you we ultimately seek. Amen.

ACKNOWLEDGMENTS
(continued)

To Anthony "Barrel" Marrapese of Reel to Real Recording Studio, Cranston, RI, I extend my loving gratefulness for always making this part of the publication painless!

To my former editor, Fr. Robert Stamschror, for getting me this far—thank you from the heart. And to my present editor, Carl Koch, and the publishing team for this work—Kudos! Know that I'm impressed.

To Aggie and all my other loved ones who make life "extra-ordinary" . . . especially Isabel, Shirley, Eileen, Pauline, Fr. Jude, Sr. Mary George, Saint Julie's and Saint Joseph's staffs and communities, and to my children, Drea and Tom, my grandchild, Andre, my siblings, nieces and nephews, and to my parents, Grace and Bill Hunt, whose twinkle in their eye begot nine, who then begot twenty-seven, who then begot seven . . . much love and appreciation for all that is. . . .

Other titles in the
A Quiet Place Apart Series
available from Saint Mary's Press

Each of the titles in this series has a leader's guide and recordings of the meditation scripts. The leader's guide contains directions for preparing the meditations, the meditation scripts, and suggestions for follow-up after the meditations. The audiocassette and the compact disc contain high-quality recordings of the meditation scripts against a background of original music.

Guided Meditations for Adults:
Salvation, Joy, Faith, Healing

Guided Meditations for Youth
on Personal Themes

Guided Meditations for Youth
on Sacramental Life

Guided Meditations for Junior High:
Good Judgment, Gifts, Obedience, Inner Blindness

Guided Meditations for Advent,
Christmas, New Year, and Epiphany

Guided Meditations for Lent, Holy Week,
Easter, and Pentecost

Order from your local religious bookstore or from

Saint Mary's Press
702 Terrace Heights
Winona, MN 55987-1320
1-800-533-8095